Original title:
Beneath the Rustling Leaves

Copyright © 2025 Creative Arts Management OÜ
All rights reserved.

Author: Isaac Ravenscroft
ISBN HARDBACK: 978-1-80567-456-6
ISBN PAPERBACK: 978-1-80567-755-0

Canvas of Woodland Haikus

Squirrels chatter loud,
They argue 'bout a nut,
Then drop it on my head,
Oops, now I'm in a rut.

The tree bark wears a smile,
Like it's seen it all before,
Whispering to the breeze,
"Watch out! More chaos in store!"

The Mystery of the Shaded Path

The path swings left and right,
I think I've lost my way,
A raccoon starts to dance,
I'm starting to sway!

Birds sing out of key,
It's a woodland jam,
Bet the trees are laughing,
At my little slam!

Palette of Nature's Echoes

Frogs croak a tune here,
Sounding like a bad show,
While fireflies flicker,
Their glow steals the show.

Leaves tickle my ankles,
As I trip on a root,
Nature's own comedy,
Witty and so cute!

Voices of the Green Retreat

The bushes start to giggle,
As I stumble and fall,
A fox wears my hat now,
He's got style for all!

Mushrooms wear a crown,
Feeling mighty and proud,
While I just nod and grin,
Nature's silly crowd!

Tales Weaving Through the Foliage

Squirrels chatter, their secrets told,
While trees giggle, their branches bold.
A rabbit winks, quite out of breath,
Chasing shadows, avoiding death.

A ladybug throws a wild dance,
With ants watching, they take a chance.
Up on a branch, a pigeon sings,
While a fat chipmunk plots funny things.

The Calm Between the Breezes

Whispers of wind, a gentle tease,
As bugs play poker beneath the leaves.
A turtle's shell, a durable hat,
While frogs debate on where they're at.

Grasshoppers leap, mischief in flight,
Wearing tiny shoes, oh, what a sight!
The sun peeks through in a curious guise,
As clouds chuckle, hiding their eyes.

Nature's Softest Confidences

A sneaky raccoon, with a grin so wide,
Swipes a snack, thinks he's a guide.
While owls debate who's the wisest of all,
A woodpecker taps, then takes a fall.

The hedgehogs giggle at the moon's bright face,
While fireflies tease in a flickering race.
A butterfly lands, striking a pose,
And hears a joke that only it knows.

The Tangle of Time Amongst Leaves

Time trips over roots, what a blunder,
Chasing shadows, it snaps asunder.
A squirrel scolds, 'Keep up with the beat!'
While worms just worm their way to a seat.

Pinecones fall like laughter, quite round,
The mossy floors echo with sounds.
And in this chaos, a rhythm grows,
As all join in, with hearts that glow.

Hushed Conversations of Nature

In the grove where whispers meet,
Squirrels chat over acorn treats.
A frog croaks jokes, quite off the beat,
While birds correct with tweets so sweet.

Leaves gossip when the wind does blow,
Tickling branches, putting on a show.
A raccoon snickers, puts on a glow,
Nature's comedy, a delightful flow.

The Lament of Fallen Petals

Petals tumble like playful clowns,
Landing softly on the ground.
They sigh and laugh with little frowns,
Pondering joy where they once crowned.

A breeze jokes, 'Your time is through,'
'But look, dear petals, spring is new!'
They giggle as they bid adieu,
Finding fun in passing through.

Memories in the Shade

Under the canopy, shadows play,
Tales of mischief from yesterday.
A napkin-wielding picnic array,
Food fights hidden in the sway.

Old branches mumble, laughter spills,
As ants parade with tiny thrills.
Chasing crumbs, they dodge and fill,
Nature's jest, it brings the chills.

The Symphony of Fluttering Wings

Butterflies dance in a vibrant spree,
Each wiggle brings a chuckle of glee.
An owl hoots, 'Won't you join me?'
While bees buzz in a funky key.

Wings flap out the silliest tunes,
In greens and golds under the moons.
Their choreography makes us swoon,
Nature's stage, with no time for hewn.

The Play of Shadows on the Ground

Footsteps dance in sunlit glee,
A cat joins in, who could foresee?
With each step, a shadow skips,
Chasing dreams on leafy trips.

Squirrels watch with cheeky grins,
As they plot their nut-filled wins.
A clumsy dog trips on a twig,
And starts to bark, he's such a pig!

The sun peeks out, a playful tease,
Light and dark swirl in the breeze.
A laughing breeze twirls hats around,
Nature's laughter, pure delight found.

So let us prance on this fine day,
While shadows play in their own way.
Each glance reveals a hidden jest,
In this leafy world, we find our quest.

Cradle of Secrets Underneath

The ground is full of whispers old,
As ants march bravely, bold and cold.
A beetle's got a tiny crown,
While worms are dancing underground!

A raccoon sneaks with socks askew,
Searching for snacks, oh, what a view!
Mice chuckle 'neath the garden's cloak,
As petals fall, it's no joke.

Leaves gossip secrets, so they say,
While frogs croak tunes in night's ballet.
A squirrel steals a hasty bite,
And giggles softly at the sight.

In this cradle, chaos stirs,
With every rustle, laughter purrs.
Join the fun, no need to fret,
Nature's mischief, the best duet!

Reflections in Nature's Tapestry

Mirrors made of shiny streams,
Show the world of giggly dreams.
A fish winks back with glee and flair,
While a frog leaps high into the air.

The flowers bloom in vibrant hues,
With bees that buzz like silly shoes.
A butterfly, in bright display,
Sips nectar like it's cocktail day.

A dragonfly with swagger flies,
Chasing laughs under sunny skies.
Frolicking petals join the race,
As nature wears a cheerful face.

Every glance reflects such charm,
In the garden's silly warm.
So wander here, let laughter guide,
Through this tapestry, abide.

Glimpses of Magic in the Undergrowth

In the thicket where fairies prance,
Mice hold a wild, jittery dance.
Curly tails and squeaky cheers,
Bring laughter that lasts through the years.

A hedgehog dons a tiny hat,
With a wink, he tips it with a pat.
Worms keep secrets, so they squirm,
In this realm, the oddities term.

A creeping vine waves a hello,
While mushrooms giggle, just so you know.
A tiny toad in splits and hops,
For a moment, the mischief stops.

Deep in the leafy, dappled shade,
Glimpses of magic are always made.
Turn a corner to find delight,
In nature's jest, everything feels right.

A Dance with the Gentle Breeze

A squirrel twirls, oh what a sight,
He spins and leaps, all pure delight.
A leaf hops by, calls out 'Join me!'
They whirl together, a leafy spree.

The flowers laugh, they sway and grin,
While ants march on, they cannot win.
The robin cackles, shakes his tail,
'This is the best, let's set the sail!'

Under the Gaze of Ancient Trees

The owls complain, 'Not our time!'
As branches creak, a funny rhyme.
A raccoon giggles, sneaks a peek,
While fondly dubbed 'the cheeky sneak.'

The bark of trees know all the jest,
Each knot a grin, an ancient quest.
With shadows dancing in the sun,
They chuckle softly, 'What fun begun!'

Whispers of the Canopy

The leaves are chattering, what a chat!
About a cat that chased a rat.
The wind takes notes, a sly report,
While squirrels debate their next big sport.

A flicker laughs, the chatter grows,
'Did you hear that?' Each rumor flows.
They share the tales, the great and small,
While giggles sprout from tree to wall.

Secrets in the Underbrush

Two hedgehogs bumble, lost in chat,
Discussing this and that, quite fat.
A thistle snickers, 'You can't fit there!'
While crickets hum a tune to share.

The bugs all grumble, 'What's on today?'
As butterflies flit and dance away.
With secrets safe from prying eyes,
They swap their tales 'neath funny skies.

A Tapestry Woven in Green

In a meadow where squirrels dance,
Acorns roll in a playful prance.
Frogs attempt their best ballet,
While beetles carry leaves away.

Butterflies hold fashion shows,
With colors that just steal the prose.
The daisies gossip, oh so bright,
About the mushrooms' late-night fight.

A rabbit's hat, a magic trick,
Makes all the flowers laugh and flick.
The sunbeams giggle, warm and light,
As shadows chase from left to right.

With giggles echoing in the glade,
Nature's joke is deftly laid.
A tapestry where laughter weaves,
Chasing woes beneath the leaves.

Dreams Cradled by Twigs

In the nook of a twisted vine,
Dreams are woven, pure, divine.
A sleepy owl begins to snore,
While woodpeckers knock on the door.

Tiny mice in a blanket made,
Huddle close, unafraid.
Stars twinkle like a mischievous elf,
Who can't help but giggle at himself.

The moon is peeking, just for fun,
Sprinkling joy on everyone.
Bubbles rise from the stream so clear,
As frogs make music that all can hear.

Nestled safe in nature's arms,
All find wisdom in these charms.
Twigs embrace the dreams that sway,
Whispering secrets in the play.

The Language of the Breezes

Whispers carried on the air,
Tickle the leaves with gentle care.
The trees are laughing, swaying wide,
While secrets dance from side to side.

A dandelion taught a bee,
To speak in verse, oh so free.
The grass conducts a little show,
As butterflies flitter to and fro.

Silly shadows to and fro leap,
In a giggling game of hide and seek.
The clouds join in, changing their guise,
Making rabbit shapes in the skies.

Each gust a word, each rustle a tune,
With sunlit laughter, they're all immune.
Nature's chatter fills the scene,
In breezes' language, jests convene.

Poem of the Woodland Spirits

In the woods where spirits prance,
They polish jokes with every chance.
A gnome in red, with shoes so bright,
Tells tales of mishaps late at night.

Elves compete in a dance-off spree,
With moves so slick, you'd laugh, you'll see!
Fairies twirl on mushrooms wide,
With pixie dust to grace their pride.

A raccoon donning a tiny hat,
Exclaims, "Watch me! I'm quite the acrobat!"
Squirrels cheer, waving flags of fun,
As nature blends into one big pun.

With every leap and quip around,
The woodland spirits spread joy abound.
In laughter shared amongst the trees,
Fun and frolic ride the breeze.

Hushed Murmurs of the Woods

In the gloom, where shadows creep,
Squirrels plot their acorn sweep.
The bunnies hold a council grand,
Debating who should steal the sand.

Whispers flit from tree to tree,
"Who's the funniest? Come see me!"
While owls hoot their ancient cheer,
The crickets laugh, the frogs adhere.

A mouse tells tales of midnight runs,
Of cheese-filled dreams and daring puns.
The wind joins in, a brazen jest,
A race through brambles, who's the best?

Amid the bark, a chuckle flows,
As hedgehogs wear the thorns like bows.
In nature's mirth, all hearts are light,
The forest giggles through the night.

Dance of the Dappled Sunlight

Sunbeams leap, a merry dance,
Frogs in tuxes seize their chance.
The daisies sway, they twirl around,
While butterflies prance, gently bound.

A beetle leads with fervent style,
Each blossom winkles, makes us smile.
Grasshoppers join with lofty springs,
As ladybugs boast of their bling.

A sunbeam trips, the dappled floor,
And splashes laughter 'neath the lore.
With twinkling eyes, the shadows play,
While critters cheer, 'Hip-hip-hooray!'

In this ballet of grassy dreams,
The sunlight dances, gleams and beams.
With every twirl and every spin,
The forest giggles, let joy in.

Embrace of the Woodland Spirits

Sprites in hats of acorn shells,
Share stories of their leafy dwells.
"Who tickled the toad last night?"
Said one, with eyes all wide and bright.

In circles round, they spin and sway,
Competing to win the jest of day.
One spry sprout claims a leafy crown,
While mushrooms watch, with smiles down.

With chuckles soft, they weave the air,
As pinecones crash into a snare.
Barefoot faeries, twigs in hand,
Rustle up the best brass band.

Amidst the roots, the laughter swells,
A symphony of woodland bells.
In shadows deep, they find their mirth,
In this embrace, the forest's hearth.

The Language of Leafy Silence

Whispers rustle, secrets glow,
A snail debates how fast to go.
The wise old oak, with branches wide,
In silence grins, its heart a guide.

A hedgehog nods at jokes untold,
As puddles ripple with stories bold.
A sparrow tweets in twittering glee,
Her chirps reveal what's meant to be.

The ants parade, their plans in tow,
With tiny flags, they put on a show.
Each leaf a page, with tales and sighs,
In quietude, the forest whispers lies.

Through shadows deep, and sunlit beams,
Life blooms in laughter, joy in dreams.
In leafy silence, we find delight,
A canvas of mirth amidst twilight.

The Hidden Stanzas of Silence

In the woods where shadows play,
The squirrels dance in a nutty ballet.
A rabbit hops, with a twitching nose,
While a sleepy owl dozes in prose.

Leaves tickle the ground with a soft little cheer,
As a rogue raccoon steals last night's beer.
A chipmunk laughs, with cheeks full of snacks,
While the trees gossip in leafy, green hacks.

There's a frog who croons in a comedic tone,
Singing serenades to the overgrown zone.
The flowers giggle, swaying with glee,
Oh, the forest, what a raucous spree!

Laughter echoes through the branches high,
As shadows prance and the clouds drift by.
In this world, silliness starts to thrive,
Happiness is the secret to stay alive!

The Quiet Embrace of the Grove

In the grove where whispers giggle,
A grumpy bear starts to wiggle.
With a flap of wings, a bird mocks the crow,
While a playful breeze steals the show.

The grass tickles toes, a gentle tease,
As ants march in lines, oh, who needs these?
A turtle chuckles, slow but wise,
He's heard the punchlines no one describes.

Mice play poker, their hands held close,
While a peacock struts, thinking he's the most.
The ferns sway softly, in their leafy attire,
As laughter ignites like a small campfire.

Sunlight dapples, a spotlight's grace,
On critters that play in this rambling space.
In the quiet fold of this rollicking glade,
Even silence puts on a funny charade.

Fragments of Echoing Whispers

Amidst the trees where shadows chat,
A secret squirrel wears a wizard's hat.
He conjures nuts with a flick of his paw,
As creatures gather, amazed in awe.

A raccoon rides a tire, oh what a sight!
With a laugh and a squeal, they take off in flight.
The thump of a thistle adds to the mirth,
As crickets compose a symphony of worth.

Each flower shares a pun quite heady,
While butterflies giggle, winged and ready.
A shadow hiccups, a treetop boo,
As the laughter blooms, bright and true.

The whispers bounce from leaf to limb,
A chorus of chuckles, never grim.
In this woodland sanctuary of delight,
Where each rustle's a joke, it feels just right!

Secrets of the Sunlit Glade

In a sunlit glade, where giggles thrive,
A fox in shades thinks he's alive.
He struts with style, tail held so high,
As butterflies snicker and waltz on by.

A deer plays tag with shadows nearby,
While the sunbeams wink, oh my, oh my!
Grasshoppers jump with a jubilant cheer,
While stories unfold that no one can hear.

A mushroom's a stool for gnomes quite small,
They gather 'round, sharing jokes for all.
The warm air dances, every leaf sways,
In this sunlit plaza, the heart skips rays.

With berries popping in every direction,
The laughter grows in sweet connection.
In this vibrant nook, life's a light-hearted play,
Where joy hangs thick, bright as the day!

The Canvas of Breathing Leaves

The trees wear their coats of green,
Swaying gently, like a scene.
Whispers tickle branches high,
As squirrels giggle, oh me, oh my!

A raccoon struts in fancy dress,
Winking at the woods, no less.
While butterflies in swirls and twirls,
Join a party, oh what a whirl!

Acorns tumble from the sky,
Bouncing off the ground nearby.
The maple's laughter, crisp and bright,
Cures the crabbies with pure delight.

Oh, what mischief winds do blow,
Tickling toes, stealing the show.
In this theater of the trees,
Life's absurdity, a gentle tease.

Lullabies of the Swaying Oaks

The oaks hum tunes of sweet repose,
Singing softly to the crows.
While sleepy critters nestle down,
Dreaming tales of the acorn crown.

A chipmunk snickers, stealing snacks,
Hiding treasures, leaving tracks.
The shadows dance in dappled light,
As day gives way to starry night.

Crickets chirp a nighttime cheer,
While fireflies twinkle, drawing near.
Under this blanket, stars so bright,
The nature band plays on till light.

In this symphony of leaf and bough,
The world is silly, take a bow.
Each rustle, giggle, flutter, and sway,
Is nature's laugh in perfect play.

Dance of the Soft Footfalls

Paws and prints in quiet trance,
Bunny hops in a funny dance.
Twigs crack underfoot's soft glee,
Nature's steps in harmony.

A hedgehog rolls, oh what a sight,
Spinning 'round with sheer delight.
The flowers giggle, gossiping low,
As beetles shuffle, stealing the show.

Little ants march in tight parade,
Planning their picnic in the shade.
Every footstep, soft and sweet,
Makes the forest feel the beat.

Nature's pulse, a playful tune,
Whirling 'neath the laughing moon.
With every rustle, crunch, and creak,
Life winks at us, playful and cheeky.

Reflections in Nature's Mirror

The pond reflects each silly grin,
As frogs leap high with cheerful din.
A lizard strikes a charming pose,
Winking at ducks in fancy clothes.

The breeze declares its playful game,
Tugging at hats with a gusty claim.
While fish splash up, as if to tease,
Making ripples that dance with ease.

The sun dips low, casting its gold,
As tales of the woods begin to unfold.
In this mirror where laughter gleams,
Nature reflects our wildest dreams.

With every splash and fluttered wing,
Life's gentle humor starts to sing.
So come, join in this joyful spree,
And dance along with nature's glee!

Ballad of the Leafy Veil

In a cloak of green, I ran,
Chased by bugs, but I'm the man.
Squirrels giggled, oh what a sight,
As I tripped and took a flight.

The branches danced, the breezes played,
A leaf hat formed, oh how I swayed.
All the critters laughed with glee,
And I just wished to be set free.

A sunbeam winked, I struck a pose,
Waving at ants in fluffy clothes.
But in my shuffle, down I fell,
Into a puddle—soaks and smells!

Yet through the squishy, muddy mess,
I smiled bright in my leaf-pressed dress.
Next time I'll take a lighter tread,
And keep my laughter overhead!

Moments in the Fragrant Understory

Among the ferns, I heard a sneeze,
Was it a bear? Or just the breeze?
A rabbit peeked, then hopped away,
With carrots stashed for a buffet!

A squirrel scolded with a frown,
As I plopped down upon the ground.
With acorns rolling, oh what fun,
I gathered them like gold I'd won!

"Watch your step!" the forest said,
But I danced around instead.
The trees whispered secrets deep,
And promised me a treasure heap!

Yet down I tumbled, a comical thud,
Covered in moss, and a patch of mud.
The owls chuckled, they knew my plight,
And I grinned wide in sheer delight!

Whispers of the Autumnal Symphony

The wind conducted, leaves took flight,
In a rusty red, what a sight!
A chorus of crunch under my shoe,
I joined the band, it felt quite true.

A deer pranced by with elegant grace,
I tried to mimic, but fell on my face.
Laughter erupted from a nearby crew,
The forest critters all knew just what to do!

A hedgehog rolled in a leafy ball,
While I stumbled and took a fall.
We created a ruckus under the trees,
Laughter echoing with each teasing breeze.

But with each giggle and rope 'round my shoe,
I found joy in this breezy hue.
In a symphony bright, with a twist and a spin,
Who knew fun could come from such a win?

Journeys Through Verdant Spaces

In tangled paths, where grasses grew,
I tripped on roots—oh what a view!
The daisies peeked with a cheeky grin,
As I tumbled down with a silly spin.

A bunny giggled from its snug retreat,
"Next time wear shoes that have some beat!"
I rose with dirt upon my nose,
Preparing for laughs from the woodland prose.

"Oh, look at them!" a bird did chirp,
As I danced around like an awkward burp.
Between the branches and laughter clear,
My heart was light and full of cheer.

With each misstep and giggly clatter,
The forest filled with joyous chatter.
For in these spaces green and bright,
Life's little stumbles feel just right!

Beneath the Whispering Branches

In shadows play the squirrels' dance,
They steal the acorns, take a chance.
A jumping frog leaps with a grin,
While birds complain, they never win.

The gentle breeze joins in the fun,
It tickles noses, on the run.
A rolling log serves as a slide,
And all the critters happily glide.

The little ants march in a line,
Wrestling crumbs, they search and dine.
A questioning leaf flutters near,
What's so funny? It's hard to hear.

A giggling tree shakes its boughs,
Beneath it all, a comic rouse.
In nature's laugh, the world feels bright,
As sunlight dances, pure delight.

The Hidden Songs of the Wild

The raccoon sings a silly tune,
While chasing shadows 'round the moon.
A chirp erupts, a clumsy ghost,
In twilight's light, it grins the most.

A wise old owl hoots out a joke,
The rabbits laugh, they almost choke.
As fireflies wink their tiny lights,
The dance begins; the night ignites.

The crickets strum their tiny strings,
And so the forest's laughter rings.
Each leaf holds tales of silly wishes,
Of puddles splashing, and fishy dishes.

The secret songs play soft and low,
For all who care to smile and glow.
Join the chorus, let your heart sing,
In nature's jest, we find our spring.

Gossamer Dreams in Green

A spider spins its thread so fine,
While chatting with the lazy vine.
A butterfly breaks into a dance,
With buds that sway, they take a chance.

The day drifts on with silly sighs,
As dragonflies wear tiny ties.
They skirt the pond, make quite a scene,
The frogs are jeering, all so keen.

A wandering breeze whispers a joke,
The daisies giggle, their petals stoke.
As twilight comes with a playful breeze,
The hidden laughter in every tease.

Beneath the sky, goofy shadows play,
Each moment cherished, come what may.
In gossamer dreams, we lose our cares,
While nature shares its funny affairs.

Stories Shared by Twisting Trails

The winding paths wild critters roam,
With mischief written, they find their home.
A raccoon tips his hat to pass,
While turtles tease, they're slow but brash.

Each trail tells tales of squirrels' schemes,
Of whispered laughter, and wild dreams.
As woodland sprites plan their capers,
The sun spills magic on their papers.

The bushes rustle, secrets spill,
With every step, find laughter's thrill.
The turtles stubbornly take their time,
While rabbits hop to their own rhyme.

With stories marked by twist and bend,
Nature's humor seems to never end.
In every nook, a chuckle rests,
Among the trees, life's greatest jest.

Echoes from the Leafy Veil

In a dance of light and shade,
Squirrels argue, none afraid.
With acorns chucked like ninja stars,
It's a veggie fight beneath the bars.

A mockingbird has taken flight,
His jokes made all the critters write.
Jumping frogs join in the spree,
They croak their truth, wild and free.

A chipmunk finds a cozy seat,
While ants march to the beat of retreat.
Leaves giggle as the wind makes waves,
Tickling toes of playful braves.

The sun peeks in with a wink and grin,
Poking fun at where we've been.
Echoes bounce and laughter grows,
Amidst the leaves, joy overflows.

The Heartbeat of the Glade

A woodpecker knocks a rhythm loud,
While bees buzz round, feeling proud.
As branches sway, they sock it to,
The heartbeat of the glade, who knew?

Rabbits hop doing silly tricks,
While branches bend to dodge the licks.
A breeze confesses, 'I'm not so sly,'
And for a beat, all creatures sigh.

Grasshoppers join in a wild ballet,
Jumps and flips are here to stay.
Nature's giggles fill the air,
As all around, laughter's flair.

In this heartbeat, life's absurd,
Each rustling leaf, a joyful word.
Belly laughs and witty plays,
Chase the gloom of boring days.

Stories Cradled in Swaying Boughs

The wise old owl spins tales delight,
Of mischief done in moonlit night.
The squirrels listen, wide-eyed and keen,
As acorns roll on an unseen scene.

A raccoon stops, says, 'Hear my joke!'
With cheeky grin, he gave a poke.
Leaves rustle with the punchline's flair,
A giggle fest fills the cool air.

Frogs serenade in croaks and calls,
Bouncing on lily pads, in silly sprawl.
Each new story flutters and flies,
In a leafy nursery where laughter lies.

This glade's a cradle for tales to weave,
With moments shared in a tangled reprieve.
Life's a merry caper, full of cheer,
Where every laugh echoes clear.

Choreography of the Forest Whisper

Trees shimmy and shake to a playful beat,
Dancing shadows twist and greet.
A party for critters, who can't resist,
They sway along, not a chance missed.

Frolicking faeries drop petals like snow,
Every twirl and spin steals the show.
Wiggle and giggle, they can't sit still,
Chasing the sunlight, fulfilling the thrill.

Crickets chirp in disco lights,
As fireflies blink in sparkly flights.
With each flicker, a chuckle's born,
Forests dance like they've just been sworn.

Whispers play a whimsical tune,
In the embrace of the glowing moon.
It's a choreography sung by the leaves,
Where every critter sings and believes.

Clusters of Sunlight and Shade

In the garden, ants parade,
Wearing hats, they won't evade.
Chasing crumbs, they plot their fate,
But lose the race to a craving mate.

Squirrels gossip, tails a-flip,
While chipmunks plan their lunchtime trip.
Every nook has secret plans,
Or maybe just a dance for ants.

Frogs croak jokes in the nearby pond,
During lunch, they go quite fond.
In between the thistles tall,
Lively laughter fills the hall.

Among the petals' color shine,
Bees trade puns to save their time.
Buzzing 'round, they play the game,
With silly jests that sound the same.

Fragments of a Timbered Life

Raccoons raid the picnic feast,
Snatching treats like it's a beast.
Woodpeckers drum with cheerful clout,
While squirrels laugh and shout about.

In the wood, the stories grow,
From tree bark hides, a funny show.
The owls hoot with a clever twist,
As mushrooms join in, waving their list.

Barking dogs chase shadows near,
While rabbits munch, without fear.
Nature's humor leaves us agape,
In the wild, it's a comical landscape.

Every twig has tales to spin,
Even the snails break into a grin.
With every rustling leaf they say,
Life's a show, come join the play!

Glimpses of the Hidden Grove

In the shade, a gnome sings loud,
Beneath his hat, a vibrant crowd.
Fairies giggle at his song,
While beetles shake it all night long.

The flowers gossip about a bee,
Who's lost his way, can't see a tree.
Zipping round in wild confusion,
Creating quite the floral fusion.

Mice play chess with acorns stacked,
Using thistle seeds to keep intact.
Their strategy's a real hoot,
As cats plot, stuck in pursuit.

Moonlight drapes the scene just right,
As crickets launch a symphony of flight.
These gentle voices soothe the air,
Making laughter everywhere.

The Dance of Light and Shadow

The sun squirts rays, a playful tease,
While shadows wiggle with the breeze.
Fireflies blink to share the news,
Of a wild party, with laughs to use.

The grass whispers secrets all around,
As bunnies hop without a sound.
In this realm of light's delight,
Absurd escapades bloom at night.

Socks discard their partners, too,
While frogs serenade with a froggy 'moo'.
Sunbeams dance to the ancient song,
In this giggle-fest, how could it be wrong?

The trees join in, with branches sway,
As heartily laughter unfolds the play.
Underneath it all, a comic chase,
Where every creature finds their place.

Echoes of the Woodland Dance

In the woods, the critters prance,
Squirrels in a funny stance.
A raccoon stole a disco ball,
Now they're having a wild ball!

The owls hoot with a silly grin,
While hedgehogs spin and spin.
A fox shows off some clumsy moves,
As the dancing beetles groove!

The mushrooms cheer in polka dots,
While rabbits wear their party spots.
The mossy ground cradles their feet,
In this woodland dance, feel the beat!

A breeze brings laughter to the show,
As trees clap hands, oh what a glow!
In this joyous, wacky trance,
Join the fun, take a chance!

Shadows of the Autumn Breeze

Leaves flutter down like confetti,
While squirrels seem so unsteady.
A chipmunk tried to take a leap,
And landed right in a leafy heap!

The pumpkins chuckle on their patch,
As crows honor their own match.
An acorn slipped and rolled away,
Brought the laughter into play!

The shadows stretch, play hide and seek,
As crickets chirp their funny squeak.
A bear does a jig, oh what a sight,
Spinning 'round 'til the fall night!

With a wink, the wind gives a tug,
As all join in for a warm hug.
In the breeze, the giggles freeze,
With autumn shadows that aim to please!

Serenity of the Forest Floor

Twirling leaves on the ground do play,
While the hedgehogs roll away.
A beetle stumbles, trips on a root,
And takes a spin in a funny suit!

In this realm of earthy treasure,
Life's little clumsiness brings pleasure.
Moss climbs up to tickle the toes,
Resulting in giggles, goodness knows!

An ant parade goes out of line,
A ladybug bears a little sign.
"Follow us!" it seems to say,
As they wander and drift away!

The forest floor hums a silly tune,
With new jokes for the harvest moon.
In every nook, laughter's the score,
Making light of what's in store!

Murmurs of the Swaying Branches

The branches gossip, sway and bend,
　Sharing tales that seem to blend.
A squirrel's acorn, lost to the breeze,
　Makes another search through the trees!

Breezy whispers tickle the air,
　As a bear snorts without a care.
"Excuse me, would you pass the nuts?"
And the trees reply, "Well, what's the fuss?"

Maples chuckle, willows tease,
　As birds croon in sweet melodies.
A raccoon discovers a stash of pies,
　And tosses one up with silly sighs!

In the breeze, they wiggle and sway,
　While laughter carries the day.
With murmurs sweet and true to their roots,
　Nature thrives in these funny hoots!

The Artwork of Swaying Otters

In the river, otters dance,
With a splash and a silly prance.
They twirl and dive, what a sight,
Making waves with pure delight.

Their whiskers tickle the water's face,
As they race each other in a playful chase.
They mock the fish with a cheeky grin,
Slick little artists, let the fun begin!

Each flips and flops like a furry clown,
Creating laughter as they splash around.
With every swirl, they paint the brook,
In vibrant strokes, oh, take a look!

Under the sun, with giggles resound,
Their joyful antics can always be found.
Nature's own jesters, full of cheer,
Swaying otters, let's give a cheer!

Whims of the Leafy Canopy

Up high the leaves begin to sway,
In a rhythm that makes the branches play.
A squirrel spins like a tire on a track,
As acorns rain down with a cheerful clack.

The birds chirp jokes in the morning light,
While ants parade in a tiny plight.
Each breeze carries a giggle or two,
Who knew the trees hosted comedy too?

The sun tickles each leaf, makes them laugh,
As shadows dance on nature's staff.
A lullaby sung by the rustling trees,
Whimsical tunes on the playful breeze.

So gather round and take a seat,
In the leafy shade where smiles meet.
For in this green room, laughter grows,
With each little whim, anything goes!

Murmurs of the Forest's Heart

The forest hums a silly tune,
With echoes that bounce by the light of the moon.
A rabbit hops with a wiggly dance,
And twirls like he's caught in a merry trance.

Whispering pines tell tales of jest,
Of midnight snacks from a curious nest.
The owl hoots in a voice like a croon,
While raccoons play cards under the moon.

Every rustle and shuffle brings laughter anew,
From chipmunks debating who's best at the view.
Nature's giggles echo and flow,
In the forest's heart, all are welcome to go.

So tiptoe softly, enjoy the show,
Where every tree branch might steal the show.
With laughter and joy, the night does start,
In the lively murmurs of the forest's heart!

The Breath of the Evergreen

In the woods so green and bright,
Evergreens chuckle with pure delight.
They sway in the breeze, sharing a joke,
As pine cones fall, it's a jesting cloak.

Needles whisper secrets of cheer,
While critters gather, drawing near.
A playful deer does a little jig,
While squirrels giggle, feeling quite big.

Every breath from the trees brings a grin,
A tickle on the nose, let the fun begin!
With each rustling branch, a new tale to tell,
In this evergreen world, all's merry and well.

So take a stroll and join the fun,
Where laughter and nature are perfectly spun.
Among the evergreens, let joy unfurl,
With a breath of laughter, let's twirl and whirl!

Whispers in the Canopy

Squirrels gossip in the trees,
Chasing tails on a breeze.
Leaves are giggling, oh so loud,
While branches sway, feeling proud.

A raccoon laughs at lost acorns,
Tales of winter, full of scorns.
Frogs croak jokes in a chorus,
Nature's stand-up, all before us.

The sun peeks through a leafy grin,
Photobombing a doe, oh what a sin!
Breezes tickle those hidden nooks,
Where creatures plot, with playful looks.

So raise a toast to leafy glee,
In the shadiest comedy!
Nature's laughter is evergreen,
As we join in —oh what a scene!

Secrets of the Shaded Grove

Mr. Owl thinks he's so wise,
But can't see the jokes in disguise.
The fox is sly, with a grin so tight,
Stealing snacks under moonlight.

A chattering chipmunk spills the tea,
Locals tease him, 'A nutty spree!'
Even the trees roll their bark,
As roots wiggle and tease in the dark.

Hedgehogs snigger as they trot by,
While the old turtle rolls an eye.
Whispers and giggles fill the air,
In a grove that's full of flair.

The shade is cool, the jokes are hot,
Join the fun, give life a shot!
Secrets thrive where shadows play,
In this hilarious, leafy fray!

Echoes of Autumn's Breath

Leaves flutter down, a leafy parade,
Rowdy critters, plans laid!
A squirrel tries to catch a ride,
On a dog's tail, full of pride.

Crickets serenade, a rhythmic beat,
While rabbits hop to a comical feat.
Pumpkins chuckle, not far behind,
Sharing secrets, oh so unrefined.

The wind carries off a nutty joke,
As a wise old crow starts to poke.
It's an autumn bash, with hats of gold,
Where each blaze is a story told.

So catch a leaf, join the fun,
Under this warm, autumn sun!
Each rustle brings a chuckle near,
Tales of laughter, full of cheer!

Shadows in the Forest Floor

The shadows dance, a wobbly jig,
As mushrooms chuckle, oh so big!
A beetle struts, thinks he's hot stuff,
While ants plan parties — oh so bluff!

With every step, there's a playful thud,
Worms giggle as they wiggle in mud.
The laughter echoes, a secret tune,
Under the watch of a friendly moon.

Fungi whisper, sharing their tales,
About squirrels caught in their own fails.
A shadowed pinball, a lively sight,
Turning dusk into delight!

So gather near, hear the mirth,
From tiny creatures under the earth.
In a tangled maze where jesters play,
Every shadow has something to say!

Invocations of Wild Serenity

In leafy shade a squirrel prances,
Chasing shadows, taking chances.
A dandelion's wish, oh what a sight,
It dreams of flying but stays grounded tight.

The breeze carries laughter, a gentle tease,
Tickling petals of daisies with ease.
An acorn rolls and takes a spill,
While all the birds seem to laugh and thrill.

Reverberations of Nature's Pulse

A butterfly flutters, donning a hat,
Wobbling slightly, where's it at?
An ant delegation marches on parade,
With snacks in tow, they're ready to trade.

The old oak creaks, it tells a joke,
As chipmunks giggle, behind a cloak.
A muddled fox plays hide and seek,
With clumsy hops, it's far from sleek.

Cadences of the Nature's Heartstrings

A lazy frog croaks on a lily pad seat,
Waving to fishes, they find it a treat.
When a breeze flutters and shakes the vines,
The frogs start singing in quirky lines.

The sun winks down, it's quite a show,
Twirling leaves dance, and twirling they go.
With nature's rhythm, all join in fate,
Even the snails can't help but gestate.

Frayed Edges of Golden Days

A hedgehog rolls in a pile of leaves,
Twirling around, it hardly believes.
With colors vibrant, the sun shines bold,
While friends make stories, both funny and old.

Chirping crickets tune up at dusk,
While fireflies waltz, all is a must.
Laughter erupts, a playful refrain,
In nature's embrace, joy is the gain.

The Sighing Boughs' Confessions

The branches whisper secrets low,
About squirrels that put on quite the show.
One stole a nut, with style and grace,
While others just stared, lost in the chase.

A raccoon once danced, under the moon's glow,
But tripped on a twig, oh what a blow!
The leaves erupted in giggles and sighs,
As the raccoon scurried, with wide-open eyes.

It seems the trees hear the wildest tales,
Of all the creatures with their funny fails.
They chuckle away, in their leafy delight,
While birds may just chirp about the night.

So if you're around and hear the trees laugh,
Join in the fun, don't miss the path!
For nature's a stage, with comedy rife,
And every critter plays a part in this life.

Mosaic of Forgotten Paths

Where stepping stones lay, in cheery disarray,
A cartoonish snail takes a slow different way.
But a frog on its lily hops, leaps, and jumps,
Finding a puddle, it lands with a thump!

The paths wend around like tangled old yarn,
A family of ants, navigating a barn.
With tiny hard hats, they push and they shove,
While a lazy beetle just watches with love.

Mismatched leaves flutter, like socks on a line,
Playing peek-a-boo in the sun's warm shine.
And a cheeky chipmunk with acorns galore,
Strictly refuses to share—what a bore!

So wander these trails where humor abounds,
With every odd corner, a giggle resounds.
Nature's own riddle, a fun little game,
Each twist in the path, just adds to the fame.

Enchanted Silence of Gnarled Roots

In knotted old roots, where shadows do play,
A gnome spills his tea in a most clumsy way.
The mushrooms all chuckle, the fairies take flight,
While the gnome shakes his fist, declaring, "What's right?"

Around him, the roots twist and giggle in glee,
As whispers of laughter sip tricks from the tree.
A spectral squirrel, with a phantom-like cheer,
Offers sage advice that only he can hear.

But just as he nods, a breeze starts to swirl,
And sends the poor gnome into a wild twirl.
The shadows explode, like a jazz band at noon,
As he launches his cup to the moon with a swoon!

So listen quite closely, when roots start to snicker,
For underneath chaos, finds laughter much quicker.
Amidst gnarled old bark, life's funny and bright,
In nature's own symphony, all feels just right.

Memories Etched in Bark

On the trunk of an oak, stories scribbled with care,
Of lovesick beetles, and a wise old hare.
The rabbit once tripped over a flower so bold,
While the tree just sighed, "Kids today—so uncontrolled!"

Carved hearts and initials tell tales of old lore,
Of picnics, wild dances, and grass stains galore.
A squirrel planned a heist, for a stash of sweet treats,
But ended up tangled in a family of beats!

The bark bears the laughter of all who have passed,
From sun-soaked adventures to moments that last.
The wind carries whispers through branches and leaves,
As each knot and scratch holds the joy that believes.

So pause by the oak, give a chuckle or shout,
For funny memories linger, there's no doubt!
In the heart of the forest, where giggles unfold,
Nature's own mind holds the treasures untold.

www.ingramcontent.com/pod-product-compliance
Lightning Source LLC
Chambersburg PA
CBHW071813160426
43209CB00003B/72